Introduction

As a child I was always infatuated with fantasy worlds. I played video games, I read comics and I read fiction. I especially loved role playing games. Being a hero and tactfully fighting monsters was such a rich and rewarding experience that I could not get enough of. As an adult, I tried to apply that same sort of mind state to my own life. I wanted to conquer the world. Sadly, being a hero just did not fit into modern day life. More often than not, I was told to just get in line and take what I am given. I then began searching for something that could instill me with that same feeling of adventure and triumph like in my gaming days. After searching for some time, I found another game, the stock market.

When I first got into the market, it was a very chaotic place. I had no real idea of how to go about playing. After some time though, trading completely without guidance, I decided that I needed to build a system to help me with my trades. Immediately after that thought I began creating a trading system based on RPGs and tactical war games. The following work is the fruit of that labor.

Special Thanks

• Cnets: The 404, Buzz out Loud, Jeff Bakalar, Justin Yu, Ariel Nunez, Wilson Tang, Molly Wood, Joseph Kaminski, Aunt Jill, Brian Tong, Bridget Carey & Tom Merritt. Thanks for providing me with countless hours of insights and entertainment.
• Everyone in the Machinima.com family for providing tons of entertainment & breaks from every day monotony.
• Movie Buzz with Peter Rallis for keeping me up to date on my favorite movie news. Best movie news on the internet!
• College Humor for providing great humorous breaks from my writing, day in and day out.
• Cinemassacre.com, with James Rolfe & Mike Matei. Some of the best geeky and nostalgic shows on the internet.
• The Youtube, Gametrailers.com, Newgrounds, Kotaku, Infomania, Revision 3, The Totally Rad Show, Adult Swim, Comedy Central, Classic Game Room, The Nostalgia Critic, South Park, Mr Show, The State, Human Giant, Blame Society Films, Smosh.com, Zombie Go Boom, Peter Coffin, Adam Koralic, Philip Defranco, Ill Will Press, Beyond the Trailer, G4 TV, Rooster Teeth, Classic Game Room, Screwattack.com, Schmoes Know, Gamermd83, Alpha Omega Sin, Vampire, AD&D and Justin.tv communities. All of you have helped influence my writing through your entertainment and insights.
• All the forgotten people that have helped shape me along the way. You know who you are and thank you.
• Drumm Farm: Joel & Cathy, Mike & Patty, Chuck & Shawn, Troy, Rufus, Becky, Mark, Kevin, Paul, Delvin, Chris, Phillip, Tony, Michelle, Tom, Marco, John, Mike, Waylon, Josh, Jacob & any others I might have forgotten. You all helped shape the best years of my life. I could not have asked for a better childhood than the one I got from Drumm and all of you.
• The US Army for teaching me the things in life I could have never learned on my own and making me a better man.
• My family: Chuck, Sherri, Steph, Chris, Hensley, Chloe, Grandpa Bob & Grandma Debbie
• My Great Grandfather Phillip Arthur Lynch for believing in me. I still love you very much. Rest in peace.

Chapters

Basic Trading

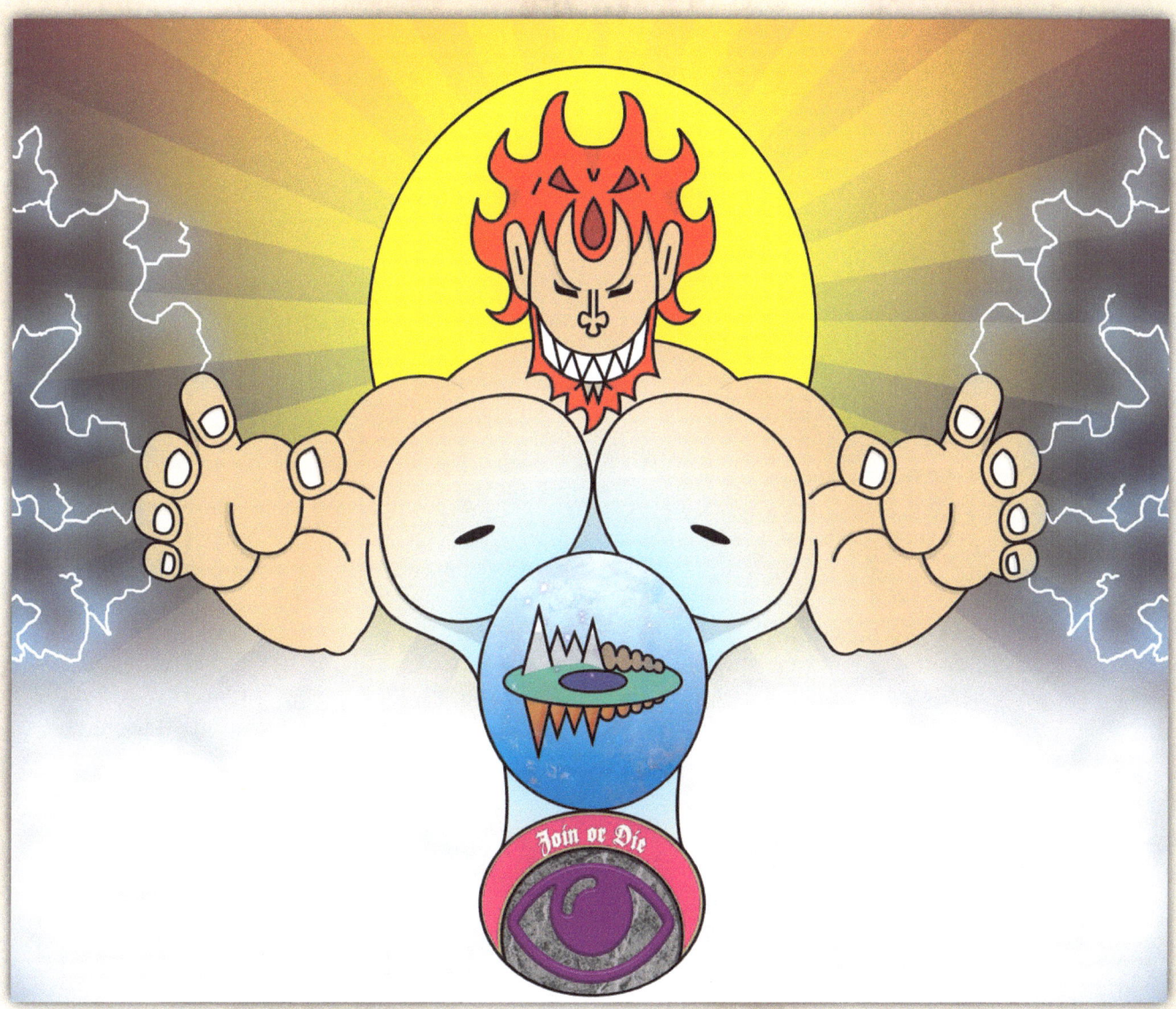

This chapter contains the basic techniques and methods used in stock trading. Inside its pages are the terms, techniques and guides used regularly throughout this book. You must have a full comprehension of this chapter before you can continue to any other chapter.

 # Getting Started

Listed below are the guides that you will need to begin trading using this system.

Things That You Will Need
1. Legal Lined Note Pads: Used to track all of your purchases
2. Clipboard: Used to keep your note pads more durable *optional*
3. Rubber Bands: Used to hold the pages down on your note pads *optional*
4. Graph Paper: Used to graph your monthly progress and for character sheets
5. Internet Access
6. Money to fund an online brokerage account.
7. A real time portfolio tracking service like Google or Yahoo finance
8. An online, stock trading, brokerage account

Opening An Online Brokerage Account
There are several online brokerages out there to choose from. How do you know which one is right for you? Usually the biggest deciding factor when choosing an online brokerage is how much they charge you per trade. Try to choose a brokerage that will charge you a good low price per trade. You may also want to trade on a margin (credit). If you want to trade on a margin you will also want a brokerage that offers a margin account.

Setting Up Your Portfolio Tracker
It is important to monitor stocks in an easy and organized manner. Having an online **Portfolio Tracker** will give you up to the minute stock prices on any ticker that you want to follow. Setting up an account is very easy. Follow the directions later in this chapter to set up your **Portfolio Tracker**.

Comprehension of The Material
Before you even start, you will need to read and have a full comprehension of this book. Then and only then will you be ready to trade using this system. Even if you have experience trading, the mechanics in this system are somewhat different from your usual methods of trading. Make sure you have a full comprehension of this book before you apply any of its methods.

Waiting For The Best Time To Get In
For newcomers, getting in at the right time is crucial. If you get in too soon you may experience a terrible drop that could ruin your entire game. It is best to save your money, wait for a low overall market and ease yourself into the market slowly over the course of a few months.

A good way to determine if the market is at a good and low point is to monitor some well known, basic need stocks for several months. Once several of these stocks have dropped a substantial amount, it should be a decent time to start your game.

Another way to determine a good starting point is to monitor major indexes. These measure a large number of stocks and should give you a general idea of the markets overall health. Some popular indexes include: The Dow Jones Industrial Average (DJIA), The NYSE Top 100 Average (NY) & The NASDAQ 100 Index (NDX).

Use both of these methods for the best results.

Basic Stock Info

With each stock ticker, there is a wealth of information you must understand. You must have a firm grasp of this information before you can effectively trade. Listed below is this essential information.

Google and Yahoo finance have individual pages for each stock ticker. (Seen above) The following information will be displayed on those pages.

1. Ticker Symbol - The letters used for a particular companies stock ticker.

2. Price - This is the current price of the stock.

3. Daily Gain/Loss - The current change in price, shown in dollar amount and percentage.

4. Volume - The total amount of shares bought and sold for this stock today. (Stock Activity)

5. Market Cap - The presumed value of the company.

6. Dividend - Amount that a company pays an investor per share quarterly. They are set by the company and subject to change at any time. (Although this example shows quarterly dividend, some web sites display yearly dividend)

7. Yield - Percentage per year that is paid in dividends.

8. Stock Graph - Displays historical stock prices in graph form.

Dividends

Dividends have three dates that are important to know: (Can be found at dividend specific web sites)

1. The Ex Dividend Date - Only shares purchased before this date are counted towards dividends.

2. The Record Date - The day the company records all of the dividend data for record.

3. The Payment Date - The day the stock pays its dividend to shareholders.

Sectors

In this book I have devised a sector system to help organize stocks into 9 separate areas. This system keeps things organized by filing several similar businesses together. Instead of a jumbled mess of stock tickers, you now have a few color coded areas that you can use for quick reference. These areas are called **sectors**. Below is the color coded sector guide used in this book.

 Boutiques, Clothing

 Airlines, Defense, Parcel, Car Rental, Hotels, Hometown Escapes

 Communications, Broadcasting, Internet

 Technology, Software, Gaming

 Finance, Medical, Insurance

 Big Box Retail, Home Appliances, Toiletries, Home Improvement

 Autos, Machinery, Metal, Farming Materials

 Tobacco, Alcohol, Oil, Energy

 Food, Soda, Restaurants

The Compass

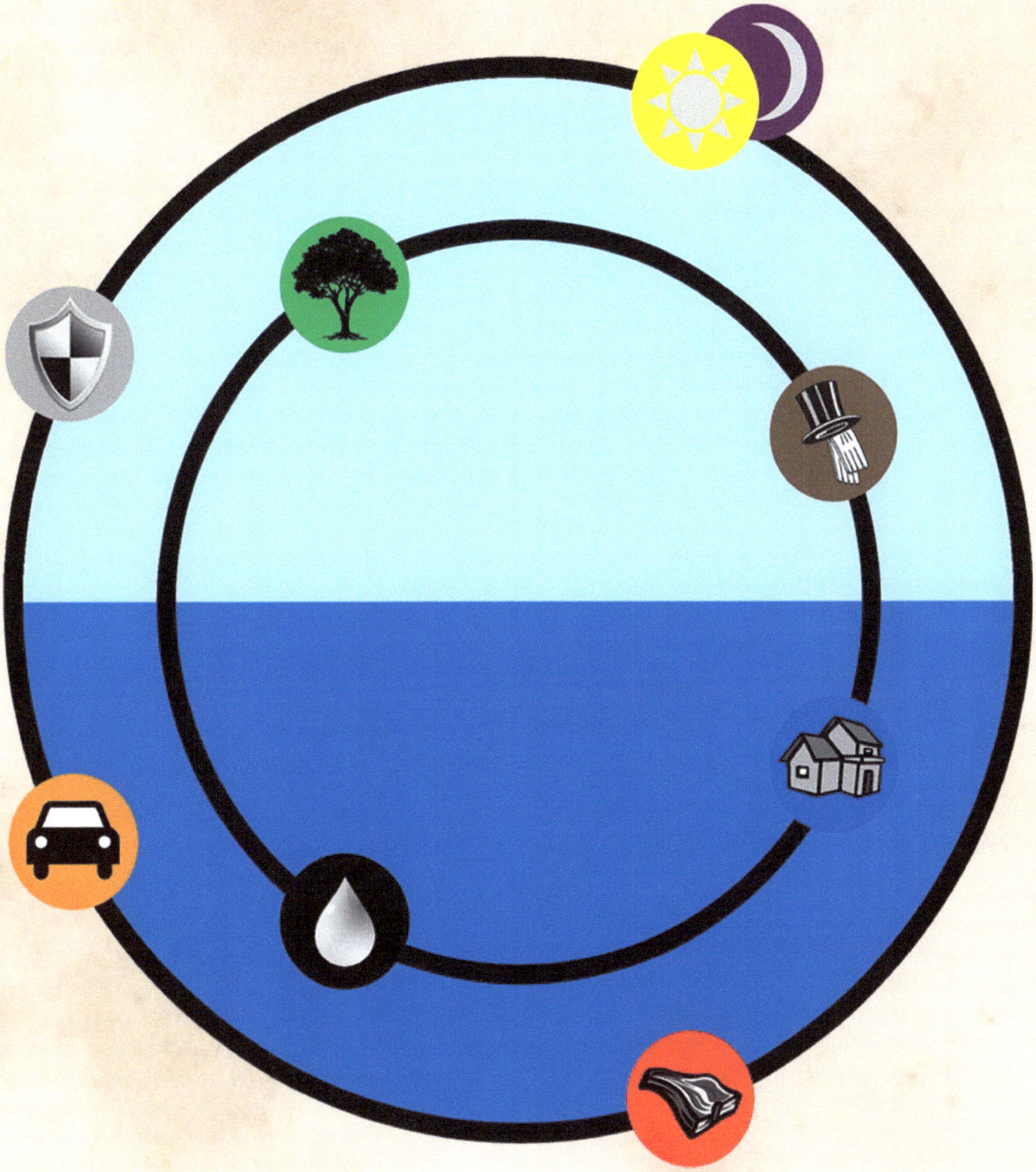

This is the **Compass**. It helps with understanding overall sector values and relationships. Some sectors are simply worth more because of what kind of products they sell. People have needs and because of these needs they buy things in greater frequency. Safer picks can be made simply by understanding this fact.

The light blue and dark blue areas represent wants and needs, with light blue representing wants and dark blue representing needs. The two separate rings are representative of the sectors that lean toward order (introverted) and chaos (extroverted), or in other words conservative and liberal spending habits.

Portfolio Tracker

Opening an Online Finance Account
The first thing you want to do is open a Google or Yahoo Finance account. Once you have created this account, you will then have access to a portfolio page. Go to your portfolio page and bookmark it in your browser for easy access. It is important that you have easy access to this page because you will be using it every day.

Organizing Your Portfolio Tracker
Within your online portfolio you have the ability to make separate folders. Go ahead and make folders with the following names: Owned, Watch List, Black, Red, Blue, Orange, Brown, Grey, Green, Yellow & Purple.

Filling Up Your Folders
Now that you have all of your color coded folders, the next step is to fill them with stocks. For each corresponding color, fill its folder with as many corresponding stock market tickers as described in "Sectors" from this chapter. There is a starter list on the next page to help you get you started with this task.

Owned Stocks & The Watch List
The Owned folder is where you keep the stock tickers that you presently own.

The Watch List folder is where you place stocks from any sector that are potential buys.

Searching For New Tickers
It is important for you to keep an eye open for new companies that have money making potential. New companies emerge all the time and old companies will often change their ticker name. Finding these tickers however does not have to be a difficult. There are lots of tools at your disposal for this task.

1. Google finance has entire lists of industry specific stock lists. To access this information simply search on the Google finance page, under the specific industry that you are inquiring about.

2. You can find new tickers simply by looking for the area named "Related Stocks" on an individual companies page in Google finance. There it will list several similar publicly traded companies.

3. Finding new tickers can also be done by monitoring the markets top volume and price movements. A good site for monitoring this information can be found in Yahoo finance's: Market Stats page.

4. Make sure to keep an open eye to the world around you. Every day you most likely use numerous goods and services from publicly traded companies. You should investigate every company that you come across, as lots of them are available for trade. Keep a small pen and pad handy at all times for this purpose.

Starter Tickers

Black

XOM, KO, CVX, PBR, COP, PM, PEP, BP, MRO, CCE, SU, RAI, STZ, MNST, TOT, DPS, RDS.A, TAP, CENX, BEAM, IMO, CASY, BUD, DEO, BF.B, JSDA, RI, COT, PTRY, ROX, SBMRY, HINKY

Red

SODA, BWLD, RMCF, MJN, KONA, CMG, HSH, BKW, RRGB, CQB, CBRL, DNKN, TR, SBUX, CCE, RT, CAG, PEP, TSN, YUM, WEN, DMND, FLO, DRI, MCD, EAT, IPSU, TAST, STRZQ, PFCB, CHUX, JSDA, CRVP, KO, DPZ, COT, AFCE, GIS, UL, TXRH, CEC, NSRGY, CAKE, FDP, FRS, SFD, LNCE, K, PZZA, DOLE, BOBE, DIN, JACK, KKD, PTRY, SWY, CPB, HNZ, JSAIY, NATH, MDLZ, DENN, DPS, DF, SONC, BH, SVU KRFT

Blue

WAG, GLW, TGT, WM, HBI, BEAM, HD, BBY GSK, BBBY, LOW, PG, AMZN, JNJ, COST, KMB CVS, WMT, UL, CL, RCII, LL, PIR, GE, BGG, MWV, LRLCY, NWL, SPB, SI, AAN, MMM, PBH, ENR, BLDR, KELYA, RAD, TTNDY, HSQVY, AVP, ELUXY, WHR, FBHS, ZZ, OMX, SPLS, SODA, ODP, SEE

Orange

F, HOG, TM, GM, DDAIF, HMC, NSANY, GT, VLKAY, BRDCY, CTB, FIATY, SZKMF, X, MT, PKX, NUE, GGB, AA, VALE, AWC

Brown

UPS, FDX, BRK.A, ALL, PGR, BAC, JPM, WFC, C, GS, USB, MS, ETFC, AMTD, COF, V, MA, HRB, HBC, AEA, KEY, IRE, RBS, NBG, WU, DB, SAN, CSTR, RRD, AVY, VPRT

Grey

BBY, TYC, BCO, SNE, BA, LMT, NOC, GD, RTN, ENR, PHG, GLW, SI, AMD, EMC, GE, HAR, HPQ, AAPL, VOXX, RSH, WDC, WHR, CSCO, DELL, EA, INTC, ATVI, MSFT, CAJ, PC, THQI, CREAF, WINA, NOK, SYX, LXK, SNDK, TTWO, LOGI, NVDA, SHCAY, LNVGY, GRMN, SYNA, GME, ATA, EAD, UBI, KNM, STX, LPL, IRBT, MMI, SGAMY, TOSBF, SEKEY, SOPK, MU, ELUXY, HNHPF, ZNGA, ATK, SKUL

Green

MSFT, GOOG, T, VOD, VZ, AMX, DIS, DTEGY, CMCSA, EBAY, NWSA, TWX, VIA, TWC, CBS, YHOO, MSI, ADBE, DISH, S, CVC, PCS, USM, P, CLWR, MWW, LEAP, AOL, EDMC, APOL, NFLX, VG, FFN, DMD, FB

Yellow

RGC, CNK, FUN, DAL, UAL, AAMRQ, LCC, LUV, JBLU, UHAL, HTZ, R, LSTR, CAR, H, HOT, MAR, WYN, IHG, LYV, CHH, MGM, CCL, ISLE, CZR, ASCA, ATK

Purple

EBAY, BBY, DDS, GPS, GCO, SHLD, LTD, NKE, JCP, TJX, RSH, CHRS, DXLG, ASNA, JWN, ROST, WTSLA, CBK, MW, FINL, KSS, SMRT, M, BKE, ANN, BAMM, BONT, PSUN, SCVL, CHS, BKS, URBN, TLB, JOSB, BGPIQ, PSS, HIBB, ANF, SKS, HOTT, PLCE, BEBE, SCHS, SKX, IDG, GME, EAD, ARO, BGFV, DKS, GMTN, CAB, NWY, BBW, ZUMZ, ADDYY, AMZN, SWHC, RGR, ZLC, KSWS, DLIA, UA, COLM, ZQK, GNC, AEO, TRLG, HAST, OSTK, GMAN

Using Graphs

Graphs are used to look at a stocks historical prices. Based on these prices, you can determine high and low trends in the stock price.

Threshold Lines
You can plot these high and low trends on your graph using what's called a **threshold line**. These lines plot average buy and sell prices based on historical price patterns.

When plotting a threshold line, you have to look for price trends that represent the most consistent trends on the graph.

To plot a **buy threshold line**, draw a straight line through the trends bottom most peaks on a graph. (In Red)

To plot a **sell threshold line**, draw a straight line through the trends top most peaks on a graph. (in Blue)

These lines do not have to be perfect. They are just averages. It does not matter if a few peaks do not fall perfectly on these lines.

Terms
Specific lengths of time are also used to better narrow down these patterns. These time frames are called **terms**.

Using a graph of 5 to 10 years from the present is a **long term investment graph**.

Using a graph of 1 to 5 years from the present is a **medium term investment graph**.

Using a graph of 6 months to 1 year from the present is a **short term investment graph**.

Within each terms date limits, try to find a time range that will give you the best possible threshold lines. Remember you are looking for the longest consistent trend during a term. You are not plotting the entire term.

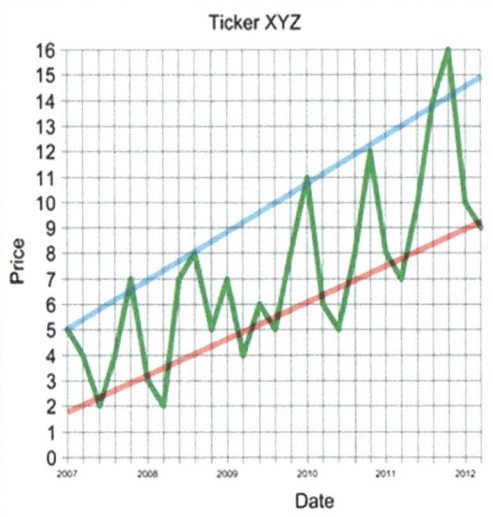

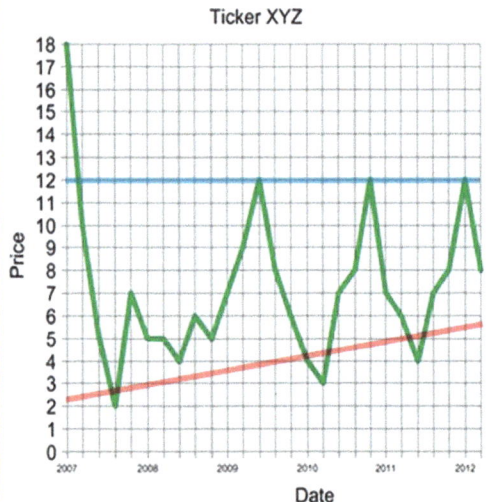

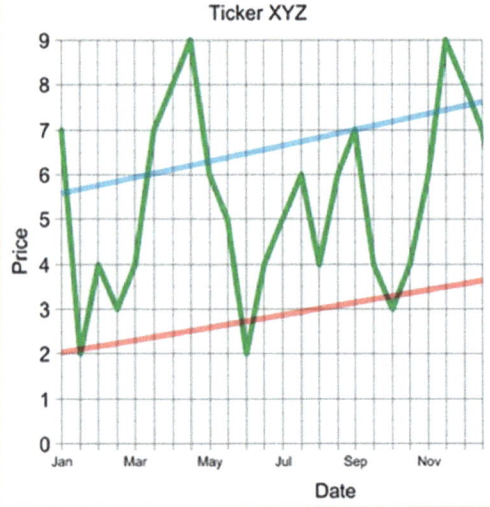

Pricing

Stop Sign Pricing System

This system will tell you how good a stocks current price is. This is done by using graphs and threshold lines. Use the guides below to determine if your stock is at a good buy or sell price.

Buy Pricing

1: Does the price pass a buy threshold line on a long term graph?

If yes, the stock is at a decent price and you may **GO** on to stage 2.

If no, **STOP**, the stock is at a bad price.

2. Does the price pass a buy threshold line on a medium term graph?

If yes, the stock is at an above average price and you may **GO** on to stage 3.

If no, **STOP**, the stock is only at a decent price.

3. Does this stock pass a buy threshold line on a short term graph?

If yes, the stock is at an excellent price

If no, **STOP**, the stock is only at an above average price.

Sell Pricing

1. Does this price pass a sell threshold line on a short term graph?

If yes, the stock is at a decent price and you may **GO** on to stage 2.

If no, **STOP**, the stock is at a bad price.

2. Does the price pass a sell threshold line on a medium term graph?

If yes, the stock is at an above average price and you may **GO** on to stage 3.

If no, **STOP**, the stock is only at a decent price.

3: Does the price pass a sell threshold line on a long term graph?

If yes, the stock is at an excellent price

If no, **STOP**, the stock is only at an above average price.

***If any graphs threshold lines are at a downward angle of more than 30 degrees, that step is given a **STOP** answer ***

Organizing Good Buy Priced Tickers In Your Portfolio Tracker

It is important to monitor decent or better priced stocks. Place any stocks with decent or better buy prices into the Watch List folder of the **Portfolio Tracker**. Remove these tickers from the Watch List folder once they no longer are at decent or better prices.

Trading Checklist

There are many things to consider before trading than just price alone. Numerous factors can have a negative or a positive effect on a stock. It is important to consider all of these factors before you decide to buy or sell. Use the guide below to help determine if you should buy, sell or hold a portion of stock.

Run through this checklist before you decide to buy or sell a portion of stock. Note if your answers are positive or negative on each.

1. Stock Price - Based on the Stop Sign System, is it a good time to buy or sell?

2. News - Is the recent news for the company positive or negative?

3. Analyst Ratings - How do the experts feel about this stock?

4. Volume - How much recent trading activity has this company seen?

5. Sector Placement - Where does this company lie on the compass?

6. Competition - Are there any other companies out there that can do what this company does better?

7. Advertising - Has this company been actively advertising its brand and products?

8. Quality of Products - Are the products offered by this company worth buying?

9. Company Size - How large is this company in comparison to its competitors?

10. Brand Familiarity - How well known and beloved is this company?

11. Dividend - How much does this company pay its investors quarterly & are they paying soon?

12. Amount Owned - Do you own enough of this stock already?

If the answers to these questions are mostly in favor of your decision, then it might be the right time to act upon that decision. If the answers do not favor your decision then you might want to reconsider.

At the end of the day, it all comes down to making a sound judgement based on what you know. This list is engineered to help you look at a stock from every possible angle before you decide to trade and shepherd you away from those more risky decisions. Remember though that bad things can happen to seemingly sound investments and there is fair amount of risk taken with every trade.

Notepad Records

Recording buy points should be done so that you have a hard copy of all your trades. Even though online brokerages usually have excellent account history, it is smart to have a hard copy for quick reference and emergencies. Use the guide below to physically record your buy points.

You will first need a legal lined note pad

Whenever you purchase a stock, follow these simple rules:
1. Write the ticker name in the left margin (There is no need to have the ticker name anywhere other than in this left hand margin)
2. Write down the purchase information in the space to the right

Purchase Information is written like so:
number of shares purchased → @ stock price → total trade cost (stock costs + broker fee)

Here is how it would be written for ticker xxx, with 100 shares purchased at 5.00 dollars plus a $5 broker fee:
xxx   100 @ 5.00 $505

For additional buy points on the same ticker, use the same line and separate the purchase information with a comma. Do this until you fill up that line.

Below is a real world example of recorded buy points.

CLWR	55 @ 7.04 $394.20 , 102 @ 6.32 $651.63 , 380 @ $1.86 $710.75 ,
LEAP	44 @ 10.20 $448.80 , 60 @ 8.40 $507.95 ,
BBY	20 @ 35.56 $718.20 , 12 @ 34.11 $416.32 , 7 @ 35.03 $252.21

Whenever you sell a portion of stock you have to erase that amount from your tracker, usually starting with the lowest buy points. Don't forget to rework your math so that your figures are correct after you have done this.

Tip To keep your top page from getting tattered on your note pad, get a clipboard and a rubber band to pin down your pages.

✙⁄₋ Monthly Graph

For this system you will need to track your gains and losses with a monthly graph. This graph will be the first indicator of how well or poor you are doing. Plotting a monthly graph is simple, just record your **Total Account Value** plus any **Reserve Funds** every month. Do not include any margin funds in this calculation as this graph is only a measure of solid gains, not loaned money. Below is an example of a monthly graph.

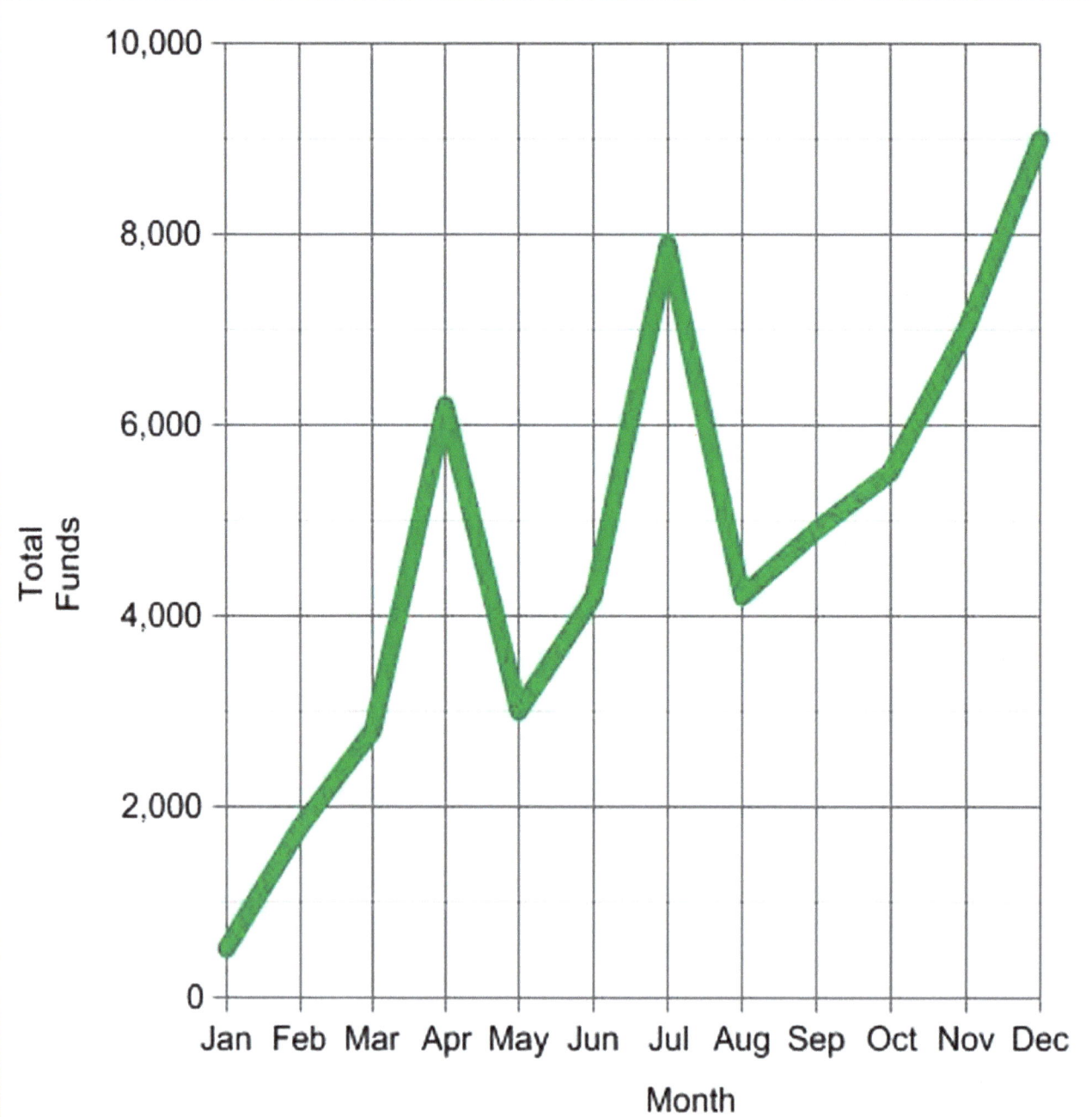

RPG System

This chapter will give you a method of playing your stocks that closely resembles that of playing a pen and paper roll playing game. It gives you weapons, armor, character stats and so on. This system does much more than just provide a fantasy facade, it gives you real guidance that helps you hone in on your targets, protect existing investments and monitor your portfolios general health.

Character Rank

Leveling in the RPG system is based on an existing, real world measurement of personal power, military rank. These ranks should give you a more accurate representation of how powerful your character is rather than just using numbers. Use the guide below to determine your characters rank.

Each rank also has a shown dollar amount. To become a rank, you must first exceed the shown dollar amount in **Total Funds**. There are no exceptions to this rule. If you ever fall beneath a shown dollar amount, your character is no longer that rank.

Enlisted Rank

E3 $3000	E4 $4000	E5 $5000	E6 $6000	E7 $7000	E8 $8000	E9 $9000	E10 $10000

Officer Rank

O1 $15000	O2 $20000	O3 $25000	O4 $40000	O5 $80000	O6 $150000	O7 $250000

Progressing past the shown ranks is only done through additional generals rank. This means that in order to become a 2 star general you must have $500,000 and so on.

Any player that reaches the rank of a 6 star general (1.5 million dollars) or higher is considered to be a god in the eyes of this system.

Armor & Garrison

Every good hero must consider armoring themselves simply because armor can keep you alive. My system is no different. Armoring yourself is done by saving money for use at a later time. You can piece together suits of armor by portioning this saved amount and using it only at strategic percentage drops in your Monthy Graph. Determine the amount of armor you need based on your play style.

Note: Any saved funds that you do not specifically allocate for strategic armor placements are not armor and may be used at any time.

Total Armor Class
The total amount of armor funds on standby.

Pieces of Armor
Pieces of armor are created when you divide your total armor funds. These pieces of armor are then used at strategic percentage drops in your monthly graph.

1st Piece (Helmets/Gauntlets/Shields)	-	used after a 10% total drop
2nd Piece (Leggings/Sleeves)	-	used after a 20% total drop
3rd Piece (Chest Plate)	-	used after a 30% total drop

Quality of Armor
Leather/Hide/Wood	- $1000 or more
Chain/Scale/Studded	- $4750 or more
Half Plate/Elven Chain	- $8500 or more
Full Plate	- $12250 or more
Mythril Plate	- $16000 or more

Garrison
If your total saved funds exceed 50000 you are considered to be garrisoned in fortifications.

Types of Fortifications
Outpost	- $50000 or more
Fort	- $100000 or more
Castle	- $200000 or more
Stronghold	- $400000 or more

When Garrisoned, pieces of armor are considered parts of your fortifications.
Non Allocated = Standing Army   1st Piece = Towers   2nd Piece = Walls   3rd Piece = Keep

Margin Accounts For Armor & Fortifications
If you do not have enough saved funds for armor, using a margin account could be the answer for you. What a margin account does is give you a line of credit, given to you by your broker. This amount is based on the total funds in your account. Playing this way of course is more risky because if you lose the loaned margin funds the brokerage can liquidate your assets in order to regain the money you lost. The interest rates however are relatively low for margin accounts. If you use margin funds you must be very careful and only use them when absolutely necessary. To open a margin account you must usually have a large enough account. This amount may differ from brokerage to brokerage. If you are interested in opening a margin account, contact your broker.

𝔚𝔢𝔞𝔭𝔬𝔫 ℭ𝔯𝔞𝔣𝔱𝔦𝔫𝔤

Every good hero needs a good weapon to smite their foes. The following weapon system will allow you to create a weapon by using a **grid**. This grid filters a few chosen sectors by using steps in a sectors market cap. Doing this narrows your decisions, keeping your targets few, focused & prioritized.

Building Your Weapon

All grids are made up of **grid square**s. These grid squares reflect your level of experience and combat efficiency. All enlisted ranks use 6 grid squares to craft their weapon and you are awarded 1 new grid square for each officer level attained. Use the guide below to craft your weapon.

1. Choose sectors that you think will give you the most potential as a whole. (Choosing sectors lower on the compass makes your weapon of higher quality)
2. Lay out those chosen sectors in order of personal favorability from left to right.
3. Place your grid squares according to your preferred style of play, making sure that no sector is taller than the sector to its left.

Max grid height = 5 grid squares
Max grid length = 5 grid squares
Number of squares up = Weapon Size
Number of squares to the right = Range

Making your grid generally wider will give you the potential to damage a wider array of targets. Growing your grid generally taller will give you the potential to do more damage.

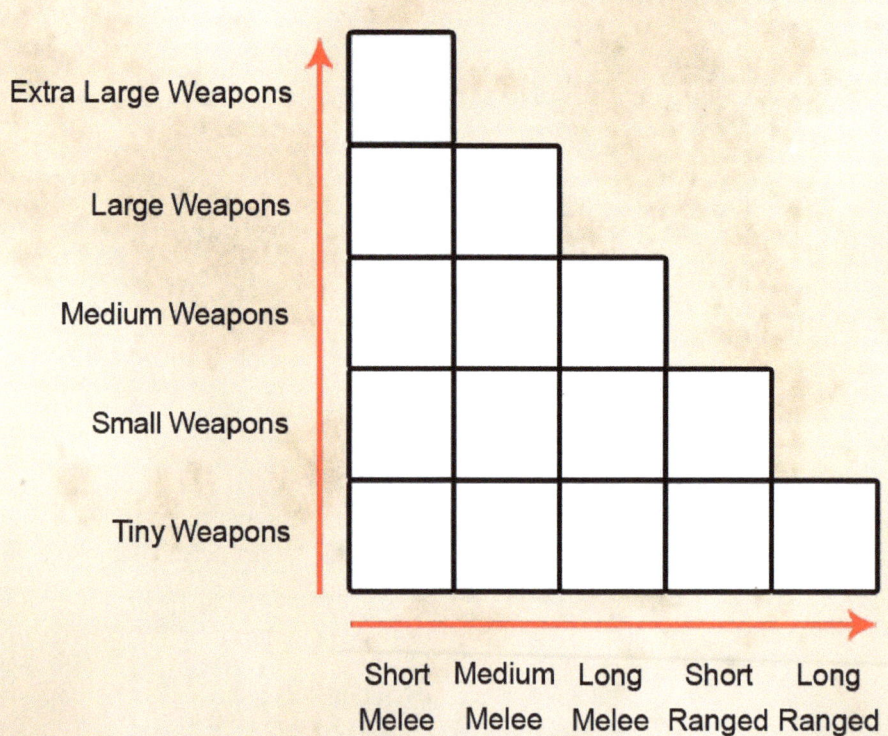

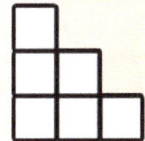

Weapon Crafting

The next step to crafting your weapon is numbering your grid using the following guide.

Every grid square will have a number inside it at the bottom guideline.
These numbers correspond to market cap numbers in its assigned sector. (In billions)
The very topmost grid square will always be marked with a 12, 24 or 48. depending on which number you think will divide that sector best for you.
Every descending grid square is half the number above it. (round down to the largest whole number)

Example Starting Grids

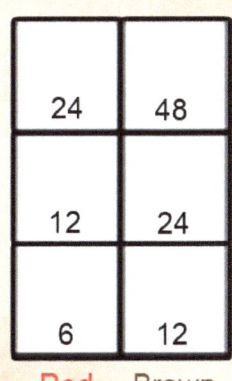

Red   Brown

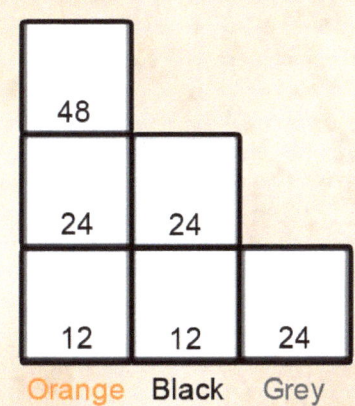

Orange   Black   Grey

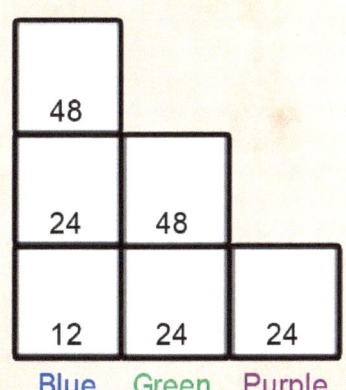

Blue   Green   Purple

Using Your Weapon
1. You first need to be ready to purchase some stock
2. Read your graph from left to right and top to bottom, just like a book
3. Starting with the first grid square, look for market cap stocks in its sector that fall within the grid squares top and bottom numbers. **Note that every top grid square has no upward limit**
4. Keep going through grid squares until you have found a stock that you feel is worthy of purchase

Changing Grid Sectors
Sometimes you will need to change the sectors of your weapon. This is fine, however when doing so, the transition period can be a very monotonous and burdensome task. This could take much longer than anticipated and hinder your play style severely. It is best to wait and only do this when you have a substantial amount of reserve cash.

Combat & Healing

Picking the amount that you want to use per trade is a lot like picking the amount of force that you want to use in combat. Small trades equate to healing actions and large trades equate to striking actions. Size up your opponents carefully before you decide which type of action to use with your purchase amounts. The guidance on this page and the next will help you decide how much money will be appropriate for your trades.

The Base Amount Combat & Healing Chart: (Below)
This chart is based on rank and gives you a good basic range of recommended investment levels.

Healing			Defending			Attacking
Enlist.	300	400	500	600	700	800	900
O1	450	587	725	862	1000	1137	1275
O2	500	650	800	950	1100	1250	1400
O3	550	712	875	1037	1200	1362	1525
O4	700	900	1100	1300	1500	1700	1900
O5	1100	1400	1700	2000	2300	2600	2900
O6	1800	2275	2750	3225	3700	4175	4650
O7	2800	3525	4250	4975	5700	6425	7150
2Star	5300	6650	8000	9350	10700	12050	13400
3Star	7800	9775	11750	13725	15700	17675	19650
4Star	10300	12900	15500	18100	20700	23300	25900
5Star	12800	16025	19250	22475	25700	28925	32150

Attacking: Naturally, attacking is more risky than healing or defending. The possibility of injury and losing a large sum of money is very real, just like in battle. The lure of a great payoff however is sometimes worth the risk.

Defending: Defending allows you to stand your ground and not take as much risk. This more level headed investment amount gives you more opportunities to counter attack later or heal. You still are in the fray with this choice but not in as much as with attacking.

Healing: Healing is a more long term approach that allows you to keep reinvesting in a stock when needed. The payoffs are not as much as attacking or defending however, reflecting your risk.

Using these levels is just the basic way to judge investment amounts. For best results, use these levels in addition to the modifiers on the next page.

Sector Modifiers

Use the following guides for the most accurate pricing of your stocks. Each one of these guides will help put more emphasis on sectors that can handle more funds than others.

Sector Modifiers: (Seen Below)
Each sector will be able to handle more or less funds simply because of what they are and what they do. Because of this, each sector has a percentage that should be applied to the Base Combat & Healing Chart when figuring trade amounts. Each one will balance the importance of each sector appropriately.

Maximum Investment Amounts: (Seen Below)
Caps on funding for individual tickers is also a good idea since you don't want to put all of your eggs into one basket. Again, each one of these varies by sector due to each sectors importance.

Sector Modifiers		Maximum Investment Amounts	
(moon)	-60%	(moon)	10% of total funds
(sun)	-45%	(sun)	15% of total funds
(tree)	-30%	(tree)	20% of total funds
(shield)	-15%	(shield)	25% of total funds
(hat/glove)	NA	(hat/glove)	30% of total funds
(houses)	+15%	(houses)	35% of total funds
(car)	+30%	(car)	40% of total funds
(oil drop)	+45%	(oil drop)	45% of total funds
(red)	+60%	(red)	50% of total funds

Character Stats

Use the following guides to determine your characters stats. They will give you a general idea of what kind of character you are playing. 1 on the scale is representative of the weakest regular sized human. 24 is representative of the strongest regular sized human. Stats that go beyond this scale are deemed to be superhuman.

Strength

1   Total of top six tickers divided by 3000   24

Endurance

1   Total number of armor funds currently available in thousands ÷ 2   24

Agility

1   Total number of tickers with buy points that have not dropped 10% x 1.5   24

Combat Ability

1   Average of Strength, Endurance & Agility   24

Height & Weight

The stocks in your portfolio come in all different sizes and values and essentially make up the body of your character. You usually want a good rounded mixture of stocks in these regards to ensure your not falling into any extremes. If your portfolio does fall into extremes, it could spell disaster for you. For this need you use the **Height and Weight System**.

•Market cap is reflective of weight since market cap is a measurement of the companies total worth.

•Price is reflective of height since price is a measurement of a companies total success.

•Picking only stocks with low market caps would not give you enough power and presence in the market. This would make you very thin.

•Picking only stocks with large market caps would neglect investing in small business opportunities. This would leave you very fat.

•Picking only stocks with generally low prices would not give you enough established and proven companies. This would leave you very short.

•Picking only stocks with generally high prices would not give you enough profit opportunity. This would leave you very tall.

Keeping a nice average of both these elements is best to keep you from falling into any of these extremes. Doing this will keep your character generally healthy.

Use the guide below, along with the guide to your left, to determine your characters height and weight scores.

Height/Weight Scale
1. Write down the top half most valued tickers in your portfolio, excluding tickers under $1000 in the process.

2. Average out those tickers Market Caps and Prices.

3. Then take those averages and plot them using the graph to the left.

Green = Passing
Yellow = Caution
Red = Failing

If you are failing or in caution it is important for you to try to guide future purchases so that you are passing.

A **Record sheet** is used in this system much like those used in other role playing games. This is essentially the sheet that has all of your information. Below is a basic guide to help you make your own **Record Sheet**. There is also a sample record sheet on the next page.

The Following Items Should Be Noted On Your Record Sheet

Rank - Update this whenever it changes

Stats - (Strength, Endurance, Agility, Combat Ability) Update at the 1st of every month.

Height & Weight - Update at the 1st of every month.

Armor - (Helmet/Gauntlets/Shield, Sleeves/Leggings, Chestplate) List your allocated and used funds for each piece of armor that you have. Update this whenever your armor funds change.

Healing & Attacking Range - Change this whenever your rank changes.

Monthly Graph - Update this every month.

Upcoming Dividends - Update this list once a week.

Your Weapon Grid - Change whenever you change your grid. (If you use a program like Photoshop, you can list and highlight current low stocks within your grid squares. See next page)

Note
Using a program on your computer or tablet is most likely the very best option for your record sheets. It allows you to update information with great ease and minimal problems. It also allows for more detailed and constant changes to things, specifically if you list tickers within your weapons grid like in the example on the next page.

Record Sheets

Rank - O4

Armor	Allotted	Remaining
Helmet/Shield/Gauntlets	4000	3700
Sleeves/Leggings	4000	4000
Chest Plate	4000	4000

Ability Scores

STR	- 7
AGL	- 10
END	- 5
COM	- 7

Height - 13
Weight - 22

700   900   1100   1300   1500   1700   1900

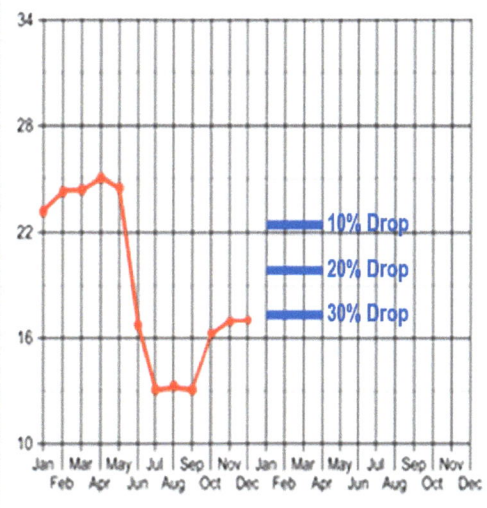

Red

MDLZ		
24		
12	VALE GM NSANY HMC	
	24	
TAP DRI		INTC HPQ DELL GLW
6	12	12
DNKN BKW SWY AVY SEE	HOG AA FIATY	
3	6	6
WEN RRD DOLE CQB PTRY	GT X AWC	BBY
1	3	3

Orange

Grey

Upcoming Dividends

DELL	12/28	3.01%
DRI	1/8	4.43%
YUM	1/9	2.10%

Wargame System

After adventuring for some time, you may want to hang up the weapons and start building an empire of your own. For these players I have developed the Wargame system. This system is only intended for experienced players of at least O4 rank.

In the Wargame System you have complete freedom to place your funds like a commander. Having this freedom however it is much riskier due to the elimination of a rigid stock selection system. Only experienced, high ranking players should attempt to use this system.

Wargame Map

Oil	**Air & Defense**	**Parks & Hotels**	**Boutiques**

Autos, Machinery & Metal

Home Improvement

Beer & Tobacco

Home Retail Soaps & Packaging

Food

Fast Food

Parcel

Medical

Online Retail & Appliances

Finance

Electronics

Communications

This is the top down map used in the Wargame. You use this map to place your units like a commander.

Each different zone on the map is logically placed in relationship to its neighbors. The size of each zone is determined by a mixture of how large businesses are within those zones and the sectors overall importance.

You can make your own map quite easily by drawing it on some graph paper, printing it out, or just using a computer art program.

Units & Play

In the Wargame System every purchase that you make is considered to be a unit with a certain rank. The more money that you use in a trade, the more powerful that unit is. Use the guide below to determine what rank your individual purchases are within the Wargame System.

Look on the guide below for the dollar amount your purchase has exceeded. That is that purchase's unit rank.

Enlisted Rank

E3	E4	E5	E6	E7	E8	E9	E10
$300	$400	$500	$600	$700	$800	$900	$1000

Officer Rank

O1	O2	O3	O4	O5	O6	O7
$1500	$2000	$2500	$4000	$8000	$15000	$25000

How To Play:

Every time you purchase a new amount of stock, you will place a colored marker within the appropriate zone on the Wargame Map. This marker is a representation of that buy points unit rank. Make sure your colored marker corresponds with the color designations seen in the guide above.

Every time you sell a portion of stock you must change the unit rank and colored marker to reflect the units new rank.

Once you sell all shares from a buy point, it should no longer be represented on the map.

Do not adjust any ranks and colored markers on the map until you have sold a portion of that buy points shares.

Unit Comparisons

This guide is a visual comparison between the ranks using traditional fantasy units. Use this along with the ranks guide to help determine how much power you will need before you place.

E3   E4   E5   E6   E7   E8   E9   E10

O1   02   03   04   O5   O6   O7
Werewolves Minotaurs   Devils   Griffons   Trolls   Dragons   Storm Giants

Additional Guidance

Supplies you will need for the Wargame System:
Miniature 7/8 inch poker chips in blue, black, purple, brown, orange, yellow, green, red & grey
A large printed game map glued onto an old table top game board.

or

An art program with a scanned game map

or

Graph Paper and Pencil (When using this option, just use the units numbered rank inside of a circle)

Applying previous chapters rules to the Wargame System.
The Wargame System uses everything from Basic Trading and the RPG System chapters as a foundation. Use the guidance below to adapt those chapters to the Wargame System.

Basic Trading chapter methods do not change in the Wargame System:
All of the things you learned in the Basic Trading chapter are still used in the Wargame System.

Reworked rules from the RPG System used in the Wargame System:
Character Stats (Now thought of as your overall military stats)
Armor (Now thought of as your armies reserve troops)
Personal Rank System (Same as Before)
Attack Defend & Heal System (Now thought of as deployable unit restrictions)
Height Weight System (Now thought of as your armies physical fitness)

Rules from the RPG System not used in the Wargame System:
The Grid Weapon System. (You do not need this system in the Wargame System since you are now able to place funds freely.)

Tips
The best advise that I can give you for this system is to not spread yourself too thin. It is very easy to get over zealous and have troops all over the place. Just because you have the ability to be anywhere means you need to be.

Newcomers can temporarily use the Grid Weapon System in conjunction with the Wargame System if they wish. This will keep you safer until you learn and are more comfortable with the Wargame System.

Optional Rules

Liberty or Death

In this chapter you will find supplemental information that is entirely optional. Using it is entirely up to you. You may pick and choose what systems within apply to you, if any.

Much of the information in this chapter was made entirely to help organize groups of people who would like to trade cooperatively. Play with just a few friends or thousands. Its all covered here.

Standard Classes

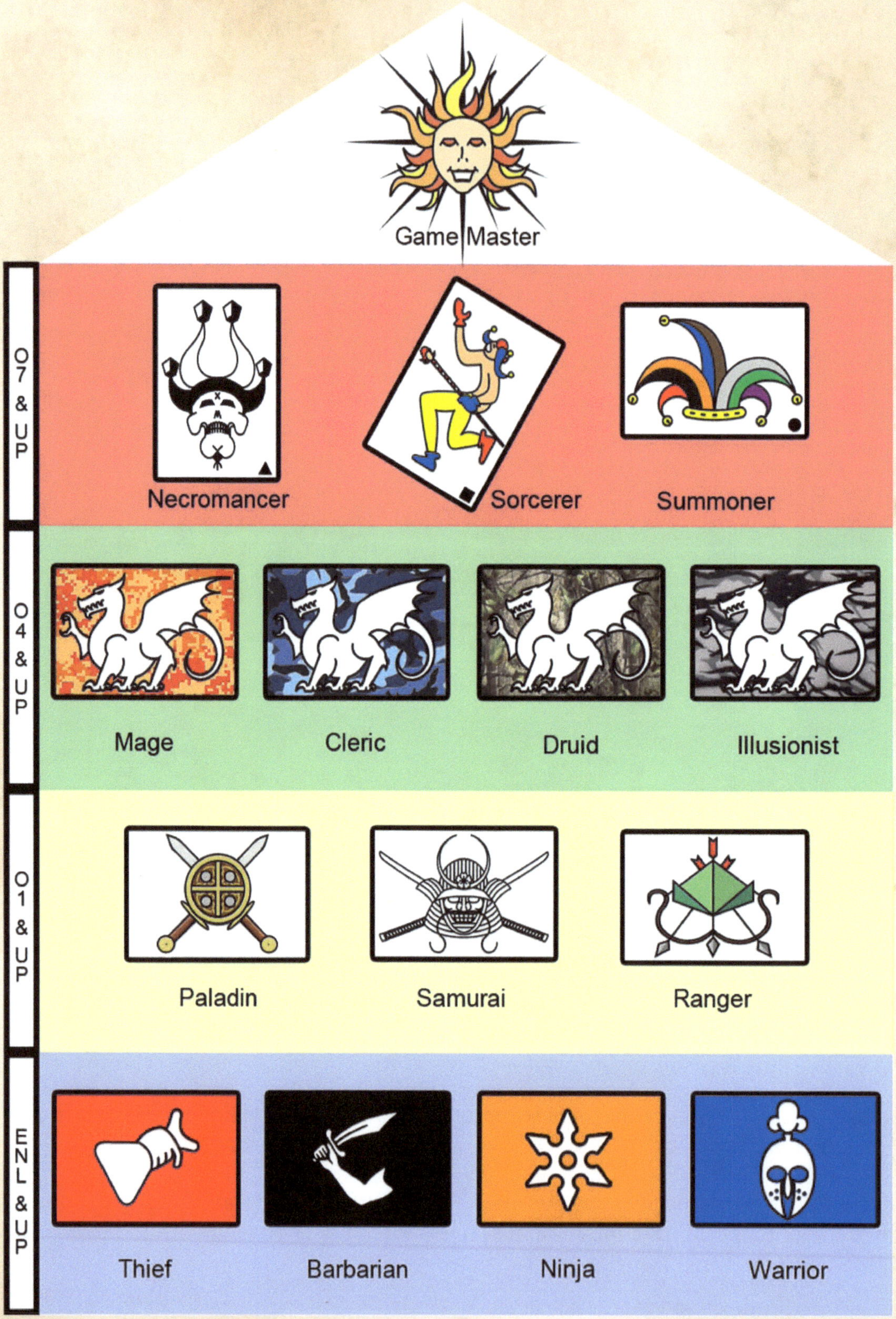

Game Master

O7 & UP

Necromancer   Sorcerer   Summoner

O4 & UP

Mage   Cleric   Druid   Illusionist

O1 & UP

Paladin   Samurai   Ranger

ENL & UP

Thief   Barbarian   Ninja   Warrior

Perhaps you want to play with a group of other investors. For these people having specific rolls to play is very important. Dividing responsibilities so that each person has a complimentary roll to play will help ensure survival as well as allow you to be much more aggressive with your play style. Use this guide paired with the diagram on the previous page to play standardized classes.

Enlisted & Up Classes

These classes use the system from Chapter 2 (RPG System), however their grids must have Red, Black, Orange & Blue before any other sector on their weapons grid. Players may arrange these sectors as they wish, however they must have Red, Black, Orange & Blue before any other sector.

Thief: Players with a portfolio focus on Red stocks
Barbarian: Players with a portfolio focus on Black stocks
Ninja: Players with a portfolio focus on Orange stocks
Fighter: Players with a portfolio focus on Blue stocks

O1 & Up Classes

These classes use the system described in chapter 2 (RPG System) with no additional guidance.

Paladin: Players with taller weapons grids.
Samurai: Players with generally balanced weapons grids
Ranger: Players with longer weapons grids

O4 & Up Classes

These classes use the system described in chapter 3. (Wargame System)

Mage: When a player prefers the Red or Orange sectors
Priest: When a player prefers the Black or Blue sectors
Druid: When a player prefers the Brown or Green sectors
Illusionist: When a player prefers the Grey, Yellow or Purple sectors

O7 & Up Classes

Each class in this system plays by their own respective systems, however with all of these classes your portfolio must contain at least %15 or more of Brown, Grey or Green stocks.

Necromancer: Uses Enlisted & Up Classes system
Sorcerer: Uses 01 & Up Classes system
Summoner: Uses 04 & Up Classes system

Game Master

Completely free play based on a knowledge of all systems, however portfolio must have at least 15% or more of Yellow or Purple stocks. See "Game Master" later in this chapter for additional information.

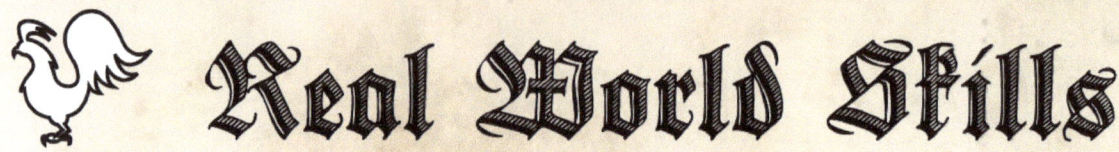

Real World Skills

Day traders can sometimes run into slow times in the market which leave you idol and unprofitable. Because of this it would be wise of any day trader to have a few complementary skills to fall back on. Below is a list of skills that are complimentary to a day traders way of life.

Traditional Night & Weekend Jobs: You want something that will not conflict with your day trading schedule. Good places to look are fast food, retail, boutiques and so on, as these types of jobs typically need people for nights and weekends.

Crafting: Soap, Leather work, Chainmail, Jewelry and so on are all items that can be made on demand. These products also do not spoil and can be stored indefinitely. Sell your wares online at Amazon and Etsy without the need for a physical storefront. The US postal service also has free flat rate shipping boxes that they will deliver directly to your house for this purpose.

Reselling Collectables: Things like comics, memorabilia, games, coins and so on can sometimes be found cheaply at yard sales, swap meets and auctions. You can then sell these items on Amazon and Etsy for a profit. Again, the US postal service has free flat rate shipping boxes that they will deliver directly to your house for this purpose.

Lawn Care: Mowing lawns also could be a good idea because you make your own schedule and have free weekends. The initial cost, fuel, maintenance & seasonal limitations are the only real backlash to this work. Post signs in your neighborhood and you should have customers.

Urban Farming: If you have a yard & adequate sunlight, urban farming could be the thing for you. Reasonably priced fruit trees and bushes can be found from such purveyors as Henry Fields and Gurneys online. Raising certain livestock such as chickens & goats can also be done in an urban environment, given your city laws don't prohibit it. Baby chicks can even be shipped overnight through such online purveyors as My Pet Chicken and McMurray Hatchery. Even if you don't have a yard, dwarven lemon, banana, orange and coffee trees can be raised indoors.

Writing, Art & Design: There are several art and design web sites that pay per job, such as Design Crowd and ELance. If you can put together a decent portfolio, you could make a decent wage. Books also can be published online relatively easily through such services as Amazon which also conveniently sell it for you through their website.

Purchasing Bulk Goods: Knives, Novelty Items, Statues, Military Fatigues and so on can be found from time to time on bulk shopping sites like Alibaba. Lots of times you can even haggle. If you find a deal, you could sell your items individually for substantially more.

Videos & Music: Using Youtube, Itunes and other monetizing options, it is possible to profit off of your videos and music. On Youtube, try to accumulate a large subscriber base, while monetizing your videos using Adsense. For music make sure to work on commission and do paying gigs.

It is recommended that any person only specialize in two or three of these skills maximum. Any one of these skills takes a considerable amount of time, money and energy. Taking on any more than a select few could prove disastrous. Also understand that these ventures can be just as risky as the stocks you trade in. Do some in depth research before you try anything.

Game Master

When a player has progressed past the rank of a 6 star general (1.5 million). They are considered to be a god in the eyes of this system and encouraged to lead other players as Game Masters. With your knowledge of this system coupled with your vast amounts of wealth, you would be in the best position to lead.

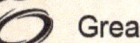 Demigods: 1.5 mil - 100 mil
Lesser Gods: 100 mil - 1 bil
Greater Gods: 1 bil - & greater

Game Masters basically function as the commander in chief for their players, putting out strategies and any noteworthy stock information continuously. Part of their responsibility is to keep open communications so that your players can vocalise their opinions and concerns. Ways to do all of this are through, blogs, message boards & Youtube channels.

One simple way to communicate your strategies to players is through a simple numbered **Priority Target List**. This list communicates areas that you would like your players to navigate towards without unnecessary confusion. This list is a simple 10 to 20 company list of your top strategical targets. A leader must place targets in a manner that will put more emphasis on companies that you would like to have a more heavy handed approach with.

Using the Standard Classes system is another way to organize your players, especially for large groups of 20 players or more. This method is also good for Game Masters with a more relaxed leadership style, utilizing this systems established complimentary structure. On the next page you will find additional guidance on how to efficiently organize your group using this system.

These systems are just a couple of ways to communicate your intentions to your players. Feel free to elaborate on these systems however you wish. You ultimately are the commander in chief as a Game Master and free to communicate your desires as you see fit.

Now you may be asking yourself why any god should feel compelled to do all of this?
1. It is simply safer to play in a game with several minds working together cooperatively.
2. Promoting the game keeps it ripe with fresh players.
3. You would be in the best possible position to help lower ranking players.
4. You could provide a powerful force to be reckoned with for your players.
5. Having a large group of players enables the division of responsibilities for everyone.

Game Master

When a game master would like to take a more hands off approach, using the Standard Classes system is an excellent way to provide structure to parties of any size. Use the guide below to use the Standard Classes system when running a game as a Game Master.

For parties smaller than 20 players, no additional guidance is necessary. The existing Standard Classes system is enough structure. For parties of 20 players or more however, the Game Master should be monitoring each players rank and play method as to better balance the party. The guides below are engineered to help achieve this balance.

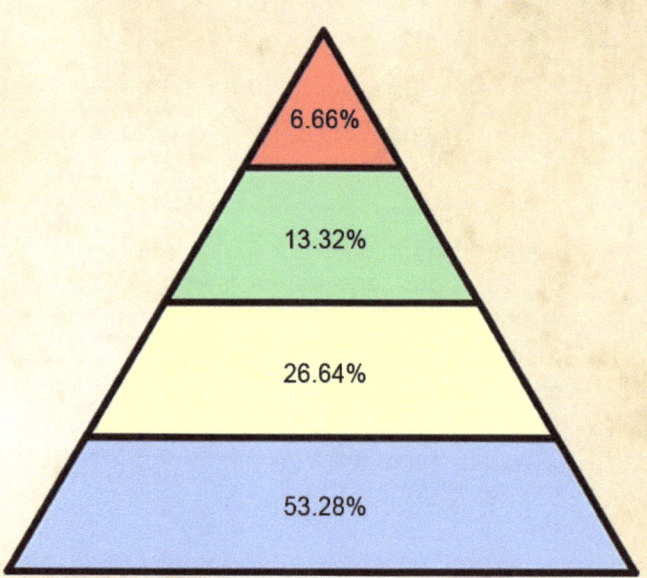

The Pyramid Balancing System
Recommended for 20 or more players

This guide will divide your players players according to their play style. (From the 4 different play methods of the Standard Class system) It ensures that your party has a good foundation as well as ensures that your party has the appropriate amount of more fringe playing styles.

The percentages of your own party to not have to be exact, however if there are any serious discrepancies of 20% or more you should ensure that players of your party take up different play styles.

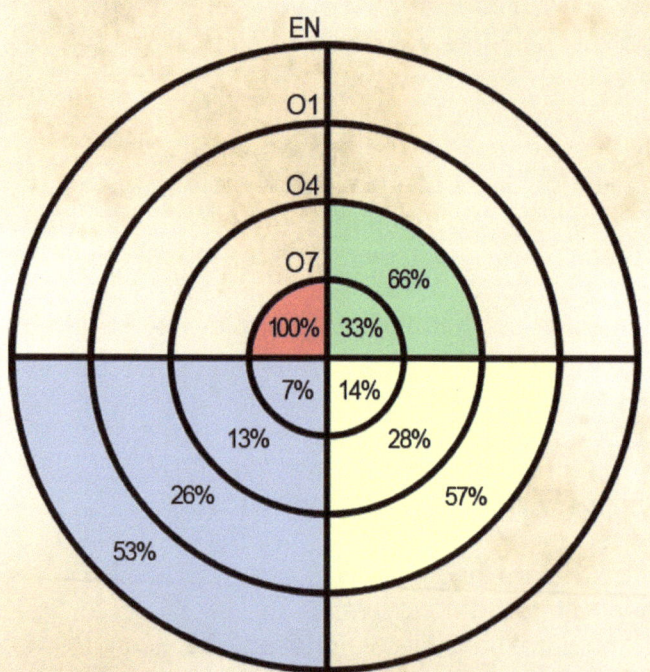

The Targeted Balancing System
Recommended for 100 or more players

The guide will even further divide your players based on rank. This should be taken into consideration after you have already done a pyramid diagram analysis.

This division of ranks between the play styles will ensure that your party is full of complementary play styles and strengths, making your party multifaceted instead of one dimensional.

Again , the percentages of your own party do not have to be exact, however if there are any serious discrepancies of 20% or more you should ensure that players of your party take up different play styles.

Races & Campaigns

The 8 Kingdoms

Legend

1	MCD	Halflings	5	CARS	Humans
2	YUM	Fey	6	METALS	Trolls
3		Elves	7		Orcs
4		Drow	8		Wild

In the context of a mathematical game, such as stocks, race is ultimately unnecessary. In the context of a fantasy inspired system such as this however, race is determined by an individual consumers actions and favorabilities. Simply, what sectors/stocks does an individual favor and consume? A good player can utilize this information to their advantage, such as when asking for a particular persons opinion on a consumer product. Simply put, if you speak with a person that fits the profile of a sector, perhaps you can gain some factual knowledge from them.

Traditional fantasy races can be applied to help further illustrate each sector if you like, however this is just for show. Just remember that they are merely labels through which a particular demographics spending habits are grouped. The way shown above is just an example. Feel free to design yours however you wish.

Traditional fantasy campaigns can be used if you wish, however just remember that this is just a personalized & illustrative way to describe your own plans and strategies. This can be an effective tool for a Game Master that wishes to guide a player through a specific path, as in the example shown above. Feel free to design yours however you wish.

Appendix A

Basic Trading Terms

Brokerage - Company that allows you to trade stock

Online Brokerage - Company that allows you to trade stock online

Analyst - Professional that judges the value of stocks

Analyst Ratings - How analysts (stock experts) feel about a stock

Sector - Specified area of the market, encompassing many companies

Buy Point - Price at which a stock is purchased

Sell Point - Price at which a stock is sold

Dip - When a stocks value drops substantially

Portfolio Tracker - Web site or program used to get up to date stock prices and information

Note Pad - Used to record historical purchase information

Note Pad Records - Historical purchase information

Total Funds - Total of all invested, margin and saved funds allocated for the stock market

Total Invested funds - Amount of money currently in stocks

Total Account Value - Amount of funds in your account (Without margin funds)

Historical Pattern - Consistent movements in stock price

Threshold Line - A guideline used to plot buy and sell prices

Terms - Lengths of time

Stop Sign System - Used to determine a stock prices value

Graph - Used to display a stocks historical price information

Dividend - Amount paid to investors when a stock has reached a certain date

Watch List - Stock tracking folder used to closely follow low priced stocks

Monthly Graph - Used to track monthly losses and gains

Reserve Funds - Money set aside for dips in the market

RPG/Wargame Terms

Zone - Regional area of the market used in this books Wargame system

Weapons Grid - Purchasing guide used in this books RPG system

Base Amount Combat & Healing Chart - Chart showing basic investment amounts

Sector Modifiers - Percentages applied to investment amounts, based on sector

RPG System - Method of playing the stock market based on role playing games

Wargame System - Method of playing the stock market based on war games

Armor - Standby cash or margin funds

Wargame Map - Map used in the Wargame for placing units

Height and Weight System - System used to monitor the height and weight of your character

Record Sheet - Sheet containing many figures pertaining to different facets of your personal trading

God - Someone who is a 6 star general or greater

Optional Terms

Priority Targets List - Short list of stocks that a Game Master would like their players to focus on

Game Master - Player who actively recruits & leads other players

Standard Classes - Individual trading systems for use when playing with a group

Real World Skills - Complimentary skills to a day traders life

Appendix B

Online Brokerages
Etrade:
https://www.etrade.com/

Scottrade:
http://www.scottrade.com/

Optionshouse:
http://www.optionshouse.com/

Online Stock Tracking
Google Finance:
http://www.google.com/finance

Yahoo Finance:
http://finance.yahoo.com

Dividend Information
http://www.dividend.com/
http://www.thestreet.com/dividends/index.html

Daily Market Statistics
Yahoo Finance, Market Stats:
http://finance.yahoo.com/stock-center/

Graphing
Create a Graph:
http://nces.ed.gov/nceskids/createagraph/

Email Me
WilliamSettleDesigns@gmail.com

Optional Rules "Real World Skills"
Crafting:
Saveonscents.com
Mysoapbase.com

Online Storefront:
Amazon.com
Etsy.com

Online Auctions:
Ebay.com

Free Shipping Materials:
www.usps.com

Graphic Design Work:
Designcrowd.com
Elance.com

Urban Farming:
Henryfields.com
Gurneys.com
Mypetchicken.com
Mcmurrayhatchery.com

Bulk Goods:
Alibaba.com

Music and Video Sites:
Youtube.com
Itunes.com

www.ingramcontent.com/pod-product-compliance
Lightning Source LLC
Chambersburg PA
CBHW050842180526
45159CB00004B/1999